# Quick Guide III: How to Bridge the Pillars of Successful Business Relationships

## For CEOs, salespeople and everyone in between

I0470575

Number 3 in a series of articles by

Paul C Burr PhD

http://paulcburr.com/

# Acknowledgements

Romilla Ready, Lead Author, *Neuro-linguistic Programming for Dummies*®

Steven Howard, Digital Marketing Strategist, Website SEO Writer, Marketing Consultant at *Howard Marketing Services*, Greater Los Angeles

Kristen Johnson, Learning and Development Professional

# Contents

# Preface

How is it that the subtle things in life are often so simple that people don't discuss them and so they don't really 'get it'? Instead, they 'gloss over' simple subtleties that, unknown to them, determine their doing or undoing.

When I hearken back to my days selling for IBM, I felt 'being truthful' in my dealings with customers was paramount. I still do. And yet when I speak of 'truth', I sometimes get a glib answer like, "Yeh, by all means be truthful but sometimes you gotta be economic with it!"

Therein lies the rub. 'Truth' is or isn't. In the above example 'be economic with' means 'omit a part of'. Yet, there's no such thing as a half-truth. The remaining half (in the context given, that which is unsaid) is open to illusion or based in deceit; the two halves combine to make an 'untruth'.

My challenge in this booklet is to convey the subtleties of truth, trust and other human inner qualities. It is somewhat metaphorical. The reason being, I want to get across the emotional subtleties that the 'facts + logic only' business books don't go near.

People don't buy into something solely because its business case is watertight. They buy into it because they can see it working in their mind; it 'rings true' in their ears; their gut has a good feeling about it - and the people they buy it from.

People buy from people and the universal currency they use comprises primarily of truth, trust and passion, amongst certain other human faculties, for their relationships to survive and thrive.

# Summary

This 15-page article (A4 size, excluding appendices) bears from my research, consulting, direct selling and coaching within global corporations over a twenty year period. The companies I worked directly for, or in a freelance capacity with, include: IBM, Cisco, Accenture, Xerox, American Express, Standard Chartered, BP and Reckitt Benckiser. During this period I've had the privilege to meet and work with hundreds of top performers worldwide.

Within this article you will discover how and why business relationships can...

- Thrive

- Fall into disarray and still survive

- Sometimes crumble altogether

I use the metaphor of a *bridge* that spans across *pillars of success* to help business relationships achieve their truthful purpose.

# Pillars of Success

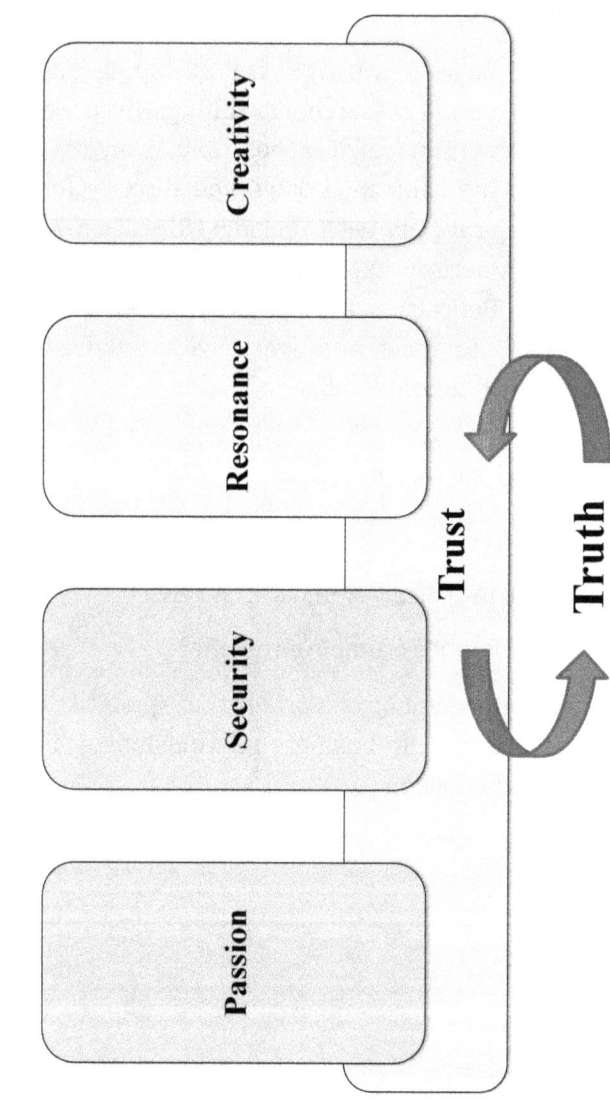

## Bullet Points...

- Building a new business relationship based on trust and value costs five times as much as extending or renewing an existing relationship with a satisfied customer.
- Four *pillars of success* combine symbiotically to support a thriving business relationship:

  #1. Passion

  #2. Security

  #3. Resonance

  #4. Creativity

- Passion and security are built by learning from and shaping the 'character' of the parties involved and their respective organisations.
- Passion and security go hand in hand with the evolution of the 'Norming' and 'Performing' stages of a relationship's growth (see *Appendix 1: The Forming-Storming-Norming-Performing Model of Group Development by Bruce Tuckman*) - i.e. resonance.
- Passion, security and resonance (*pillars #1, #2 and #3*) are prerequisites to foster creativity (*pillar #4*).
- These four *pillars* support the pathway across the *bridge* to reach the relationship's destination, its purpose.
- The *pillars* are embedded in a *foundation stone* of trust. Each and all the *pillars* may crumble and fall

but can be rebuilt as long as their foundation, trust, remains intact.

- Much deeper than trust, exists truth. It permeates the structure of the *bridge*, its beginning and its destination. Not-truth, falsity and illusion, destroy the *bridge*.
- Business relationships don't end by themselves. They end when their purpose is achieved or deemed unachievable.
- 'Throwing in the towel' though, especially for a large investment decision, is sometimes seen as 'political suicide'. The ensuing relationship becomes moribund. The flaws in (and all learning from) the original decision making process are swept under the 'corporate carpet'.
- The best time to end the current structure of a relationship is when it is running perfectly - so that you can renew it at a stronger level.

———

## Logic, Premium and Legacy

Volumes I and II of this series of *Quick Guides to Business* focused primarily on how, from the outset, top salespeople forge business relationships differently from moderate performers. This volume picks up from where Volume II leaves off, to describe what needs to happen for medium and long-term relationships to thrive.

The same principles apply to any relationship, be it business or personal, many-to-many or one-to-one - between 'you' (by 'you' I mean you, me, we, us) and your boss, peers, direct reports, customers, best friend or partner. In this article, I'll focus primarily on two contexts...

1. Complex B2B sales-customer relationships - and
2. Executive leadership in business transformation

Both typify large-network, many-to-many relationships.

## Logic - less cost

Research shows that once you've established a customer relationship based on mutual trust and value, it takes five times the effort to build the same relationship with a new customer as it does to maintain it with your current customer.

When the *cost* of new prospect sales is *five times* that of existing satisfied customer sales, you don't need a certificate in mathematics to appreciate the importance of satisfying, if not exceeding, the expectations of existing customers irrespective of the premium you earn from brand loyalty.

## Premium - higher earnings

A reputable brand image makes selling a lot easier. I had no problem whatsoever getting to see new clients when I worked for IBM. Cold-calling for an organisation that isn't a 'household' name, however, was a real 'eye-opener' for me after I made the switch.

The value of your reputation is the premium that customers will pay to do business with you over and above what they will pay your competitors, all else being equal, plus the cost reduction in sales your brand reputation affords you.

**A simple example:** 'Household-name', supplier *A*, renowned for its high quality products and services, sells a PC. 'Relatively-unknown' supplier, *B*, clones *A's* PC with the exact same components, guarantees and terms of service. Intrinsically there's no difference between PCs from either supplier. The cost of production and distribution of each product is the same.

Look at the buying/selling process from a customer perspective. All else being equal...

- What price difference will a customer pay (for the increased: reassurance, sense of status or another emotional, differential source of value they feel) for a PC from supplier *A* over supplier *B*?
- Reduction in sales cycle time and resourcing: how quicker and easier is it for a seller to convince a customer of the quality of a PC from supplier A compared with supplier B?

*Brand value = [(what customers pay you) - (what customers pay for the exact same product/service from your competitors)] + (increase in productivity/cost-reduction in sales afforded by your brand)*

## Legacy - higher contribution

How do you want to look back on your time in sales and management at the end of your career? How do you want to be remembered? As a seller, buyer or leader: do you want to feel you've kept (or at least strived to keep) the agreements you made?

Maybe a business world forged with 100% truthful relationships is somewhat of a pipe dream, but as you look at the world's economy and the 'wars' for limited resources right now, what choice do we have? And we have to imagine something before necessity will mother its invention - do we not?

'You' can either contribute to a world where wealth and power are shared through equitable negotiation - or not, truth or illusion/deception, abundance or scarcity, oneness or separateness, love or fear. 'You' choose! (But this is the topic contained in another book of mine, *Defrag your Soul*.)

———

# Thrive, Survive or Crumble

Consider *four pillars of success* for a business relationship to achieve its purpose:

#1. Passion

#2. Security

#3. Resonance

#4. Creativity

The *pillars* are built on a *foundation* of trust. Collectively they support a *bridge* (a path across a *chasm*) to achieve its purpose (at *the other side*). The *bridge* is built from trust, passion, security, resonance, creativity, purpose and each individual's 'personal truth'.

*Personal truth: the supreme reality and consequences of how you feel inside, your intentions, the actions you take and from whence they are borne, from passion or from fear.*

Before we look at each *pillar*, let us start with the reason for the relationship, its purpose.

## Purpose

From an individual perspective, the *bridge* overarches and is also compromised of each individual stakeholder's desires (the *bricks*) to achieve (cross a *chasm* to) the 'greater good'. If I may stretch the metaphor further, a business relationship is the *mortar* that cements the *bricks* together. When the bricks fit

8

neatly together and are plumb, the stronger the bond and more durable stands the *bridge*.

Purpose is thus subjective and personal. It depends on whether you focus on the destination you think the *bridge* leads to, or the individual components (*bricks*) that motivate you to collaborate in building the *bridge*.

Purpose answers the questions: *"What's in it for us?"* and *"What's in it for me?"* for everyone involved.

From an organizational perspective, two or more organisations come together to create an outcome that they can't create on their own; at least not as quickly or effectively. Each organisation possesses a network of stakeholders, each with their own personal outcomes from the relationship. The collective purpose ('greater good') is congruent with and differs from the purposes that each organisation has for the relationship. These organisational purposes are, in turn, congruent with individual stakeholders' purposes.

For example, a major B2B services deal, between two large corporations, will have many perspectives: the buyers, the sellers, the installers, as well as the views of internal (e.g. directors not involved directly in the deal) and external (e.g. shareholders, industry analysts, customers) stakeholders.

Imagine a large and complex services deal is signed. The first task is to confirm and align expectations of those:

1. Whose job or influence will be impacted by that which was sold - the planners and those who will cross the *bridge*
2. Who will deliver the 'business solution' - the builders of the *bridge*
3. Who sold the 'solution' - the chief architects
4. Who bought the 'solution' - the eventual owners of the *bridge*
5. External and interested *onlookers* - viewing the *bridge* from a distance.

At this stage, it's best that any missed 'devil in the detail' rears its head and makes itself known. The sooner any misperceptions or conflicts in perception are resolved, often the less costly the consequences, either financially or in loss of trust.

For those who have seen the movie, *Bridge over the River Kwai*, the metaphor proves valid. It wasn't until all the conflicts and misperceptions had been resolved could the bridge be built - and, in this instance, in a completely different location.

Back to business: imagine that a sales team oversells and sets expectations above or beyond what the delivery or customer's recipient team have budgeted for. As a result, either the project 'under-delivers' or comes in way over budget. In my experience, it often does so at the forfeiture of the selling organisation; to avoid contractual dispute and/or the customer losing trust in the seller.

Expectations (e.g. profit expectations, customer service expectations, problem resolution expectations or relationship expectations) are not met for one of or both the selling and buying organisations. Such a downgrading will threaten the integrity of the pillars of success or worse still, destabilise the *bridge's* foundations altogether.

**Congruence** (see illustration overleaf):

For a relationship to thrive, over and above the contracted measures of success, it's vital to align the various stakeholders' perceptions of (the *bridge*) and expectations from (the *destination*) what you have sold. Ideally, do this upfront; during the selling process before the project commences - or as soon as is feasible thereafter. Once you have achieved a large degree of congruence, keep it that way!

Back to the metaphor: congruence, upfront, means every stakeholder sees the same *plans for the bridge;* their expectations are aligned. Each may be studying a particular facet of its *structure* or the whole *bridge* itself. Congruence implies there are no distorted views. Everyone sees the same *bridge* in their mind whether they study it with a telescope or microscope.

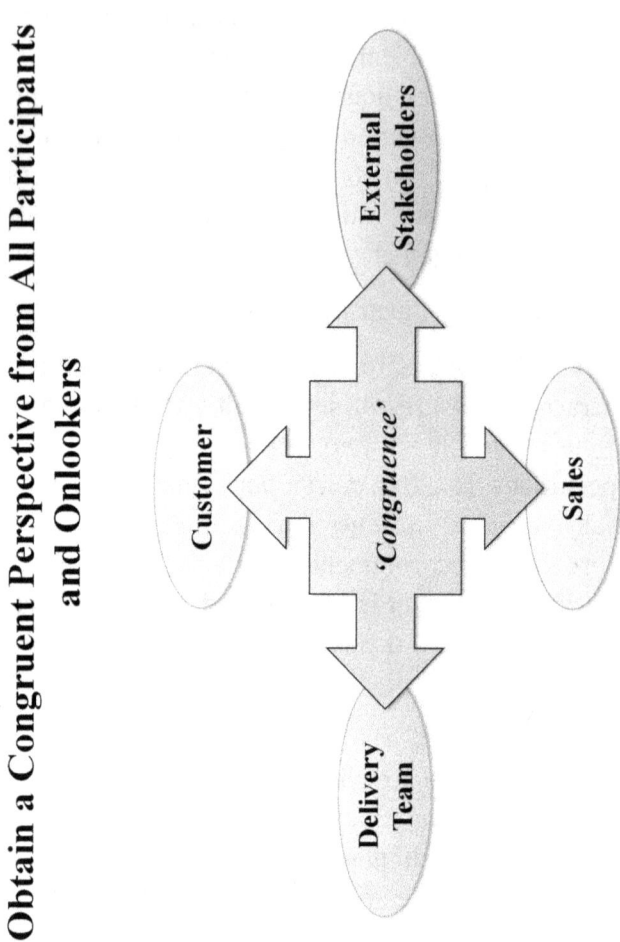

**Obtain a Congruent Perspective from All Participants and Onlookers**

With 'upfront congruence' achieved, the task now prevails to build the *bridge* to specification.

## Pillar #1: Passion

Passion energises the life force of the relationship. Top salespeople have a passion for customer value and the outcome. Once the relationship has started it requires a passion, by all involved, for the journey as much as the destination.

In its purest form, 'real passion' is 'love'; not a word conventionally associated with business apart from when it is used as a verb (I 'love'...) to replace 'really like' or 'feel passionate about'. Real passion (love) is more than that. It implies truth.

*Truth is love is truth. All that is untrue (deceit or illusion) is not love, not real passion.*

When I talk about passion, I talk of the commitment to truth: to learn from successes and setbacks truthfully and to resolve issues truthfully. When things go better than expected (or awry), to share the proceeds (or renegotiate) honestly.

The truth reveals wisdom but it often takes courage or willpower to apply that wisdom. It takes a 'faith-in-self' to resolve issues without knowing the answers in advance. (I list *7 key traits* of top salespeople, of which 'passion' and 'faith-in-self' are two, in *Quick Guide II: How to Spot, Mimic and Become a Top Salesperson*.)

*Faith-in self = willpower + commitment + self trust*

*Truth is the path upon which, when you walk, you become the path - so that others will follow.*

And

*Passion = faith-in-self to find, become and live truth.*

## Pillar #2: Security

In modern day business parlance, the term 'security' is often used synonymously with 'safety' and 'compliance'. I will add to these definitions with the phrase, *secure in knowledge and self.* In ancient wisdom, 'secure' meant something different to locks, firewalls and safety standards. It's worth looking at its etymological roots...

The messenger of the wisdom of the gods was *Mercury*. *La Mer* is the French noun for 'sea' - which links phonetically to 'see'. *'...Cury'* links to cure (or healing) which stems from the phrase 'to make whole'. Cure is not that far away from 'la coeur', the heart; in this case, 'the heart of the matter'.

*Mercury = see + cure = see how to make whole or, better still, make as one.*

Putting this all together...

*Security is about seeing the heart of the matter (relationship) and feeling (or better still knowing) that its purpose will be achieved.*

A pervasive sense of 'security' has a symbiotic connection with the passion everyone has for the success of a relationship and the journey required. Should a sense of insecurity in the business relationship develop - i.e. its *pillar* develops a fault - the *pillar* is repaired by delving into the truth of the matter.

Here is a self-coaching tool I use with executive clients to build passion and develop a sense of security for strategic change programmes they are about to embark upon (or have already started). I used it with the European General Manager of a large US organisation. He was given a directive to transform the company from a 'leading product' to a 'leading services' supplier. His major challenge was that the national management teams of the European countries saw all such US initiatives as veiled 'cost cutting exercises' and that Americans had no appreciation for the idiosyncrasies peculiar to each of Europe's national markets. The General Manager used this tool (along with others from a kitbag of self-coaching tools) to scope the change programme that he knew he had to sell consultatively to his management teams. He knew from experience that simply telling them to make the changes would prove fruitless.

I am not at liberty to go into the detailed answers my client came up with. Rather, I use this example so you can appreciate the complexity of the context in which this tool can be used effectively.

Author's note: This self-coaching tool is inspired by the original works of Professor Chris Argyris, *Harvard Business Review*, September 1997, *Double Loop Learning in Organizations* and following publications.

———

*Tip: It was from Professor Argyris's works that I first learned to use the word, 'setback', instead of 'failure'. Professor Argyris found that whilst people wax lyrically about their 'successes', they are prone to clam up when asked about their 'failures'. 'Setback' proves a far less emotive word.*

———

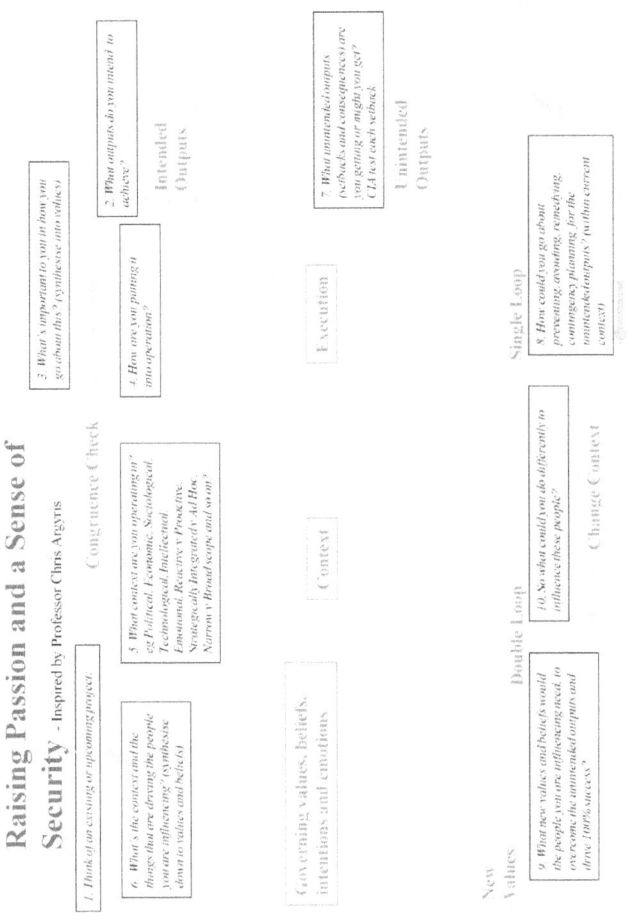

This tool typically takes an individual client an hour to go through. It is best completed in one sitting, the first time around. Find somewhere quiet where you won't be disturbed. After the first-time-completion, you can then develop it iteratively as you put your influencing strategies into practice. It can also be used in teams, in which case half a day or more may be required.

Complete the following and record any ancillary thoughts you have during the process...

1. *Describe in one sentence an existing or upcoming project*
2. *What outputs/outcomes do you intend to achieve? That is, what will success look like in terms of finance, people, resources, relationships, actions, learning, skills development, feelings, values, beliefs and environmental changes?*

   (Author's note: I intend to devote my next business guide to a personal/corporate measurement scorecard that delves into key missing pieces from traditional business scorecards.)

3. *What's important to you in how you go about this? Synthesise your answer into short 'value-statements', ideally single or double word values, e.g. financial viability, trust, equitable handling.*
4. *How are you putting the project into operation? List the major action steps and milestones by which you intend to achieve your outcomes. Include with whom you will engage and how. What will you do specifically to forge the relationships with key stakeholders necessary to succeed?*
5. *Describe the context in which you are operating. For example: environmental factors (political, economic, sociological, technological and emotional), major changes (internal and external), reactively or*

   *proactively, strategically integrated or ad hoc, narrowly or broadly in scope, and so on. Is there any conflict with your answers to Question 3?*

6. *Over and above the answer to Question 5, describe the context and the things that are specifically driving the people you seek to influence. Once again, synthesise your answer into short statements - e.g. economic factors, recent/projected business results, trust or fear, optimism or cynicism, truth, illusion or deceit. Focus specifically on people who (may) lack passion or lack a sense of security about the project's success.*

   *Answer specifically...*

   a. *What does each of these people really want?*

   b. *What innermost fears hold each of them back or stifle their commitment?*

   c. *Is there any conflict in the answers to a and b with your answers to Questions 3 and 5?*

7. *What unintended outputs (i.e. setbacks and their consequences) are you getting or might you get? This is your opportunity to list everything that could go wrong with your strategy e.g. the economy may take a further downturn, stakeholders won't buy into the strategy, you don't get sufficient funding, etc. Once again, focus specifically on people who (may) display a lack of passion or sense of insecurity about the project's success.*

————

   *Tip: To begin with, keep each (potential or existing) 'setback' in thought only, no further. Avoid dwelling in the feeling of each setback. Instead, place each setback, one-by-one, in its own imaginary bubble. Go in and experience the contents of each bubble fleetingly. As you leave each bubble, detach your emotions from its contents.*

———

*Give each unintended output (what is commonly known as) 'the CIA (Control, Influence or Accept) test'. Mark each as a C, I or an A.*

*C- Is it ͟controllable?*

*I - Can I ͟influence (i.e. lessen the likelihood) this outcome? or*

*A - Do I have to ͟accept that it is not realistically under my control (e.g. economic downturn)?*

8. *According to each respective C, I or A category: how could you go about preventing (head off at the pass), avoiding (circle around), remedying (heal or make whole), contingency planning for or defending against each of the unintended outputs in Question 7 (within current context listed in Questions 3, 5 and 6)?*

9. *What new values, beliefs, intentions and emotions would the people you are influencing need to develop, to overcome the unintended outputs and drive 100% success (include: collective buy in, willingness to explore the unknown, security, passion!)?*

10. *What could you do differently to influence these people to take on these new, more enabling values,*

> *beliefs, intentions and emotions listed in Question 9?*
> *What specifically could you do to raise their passion*
> *for and sense of security in the project?*

The most valuable aspect of this tool is that it helps you to appreciate and bring into alignment (as much as possible) the mindsets and motivations of all the key stakeholders who could stop or threaten the project's success. The process helps you 'tune-in' to, and shapes your influencing strategy to raise, each stakeholder's passion for and sense of security about the project's success.

By 'tuning-in' to each stakeholder, you *prepare the ground* to construct *pillar #3*.

# Pillar #3: Resonance

*"People like people like themselves"* - most of the time. There's another phrase from ancient wisdom, "*Tyrants attract pacifists and pacifists attract tyrants"*. You see a certain level of cooperation in both types of relationships, each with differing dynamics and consequences. Let's start with the 'like-like' condition.

### Like for Like People

Some describe resonance as being on the same wavelength--being in tune with one another, two or more instruments forming a melodic harmony. The sum of the individual notes combines to make an orchestral sound, far richer than the sum of their parts.

In business relationships, staying in tune with one's partners requires sensibility. Another of the *7 key traits* by which you discern a top performer from a moderate (see *Quick Guide II: How to Spot, Mimic and Become a Top Salesperson*).

*Sensibility means we understand how someone else feels and why - especially when their logic, reasoning, intentions, feelings and emotions differ from our own. When we understand our own logic, reasoning, intentions, feelings and emotions - then we can adapt and make a connection.*

I use a framework to help clients understand the thinking preferences behind the logic and reason they demonstrate to others - and vice versa. Some...

- Prefer big picture; others prefer attention-to-detail.
- Believe in (albeit extreme) achievement-at-any-cost; others put people's trust and well-being first.
- Abhor ambiguity; others thrive on it and see it as an opportunity to create something (join the dots-of-the-unknown) that no one else has done before.

The preferences are many-fold. I don't discuss them in terms of right or wrong. Instead I get clients to consider what's important over the long term; what will work and what won't.

Preferences are not competencies. They indicate how we like to think and talk about things. Some of our aspirations, and the logic and reasoning we use to achieve them, will be apparent; some may be just below the surface. In the depths below lie our innermost aspirations and fears. Some of these are within our consciousness, others are subconscious.

Tuning into these innermost aspirations and fears requires a newer generation of probing-and-influencing-with-integrity tools. It's about going to a space in someone's psyche that is shielded from the outside world. The shield protects these hidden emotions from outsiders. However, there is a door with an admission price: it's called *trust* and is borne of *truth*. More about trust and truth will follow.

## Tyrants and Pacifists

I've seen research that compared the efficacy of two naval shipyards. One commander preferred a direct-control approach with a modicum of consultation. The second commander applied a highly consultative approach. Both shipyards ran equally efficient production lines. The one thing they had in common was that people worked happily in the environment they preferred to be in. The first shipyard's people preferred working to direct orders; the second group preferred more freedom to make their own decisions. This was verified when the commanders switched positions and production levels at both shipyards fell off. When they switched back, the respective 'resonances' with their people and original productivity levels were restored.

Tyrants and pacifists, on the other hand, have an essentially dissonant relationship. Pacifists allow tyrants to control a relationship because of a lack of self trust. They do not trust themselves to make decisions and so they concede their power; thereby hoping to avoid (self) blame should things not go according to plan.

Tyrants control conciliatory pacifists for an analogous reason. They do not trust themselves either, to put their trust in others and so they take control of the relationship. They attempt to shine like the sun, but their light is of a false sun. A real sun radiates fire and passion into the hearts and minds of others; a false sun instils compliance, a tick-in-the-box mentality and approach, borne of fear. And fear breeds deception, falsity, illusion, not-truth and not-passion.

Without passion (*pillar #1*) there is little, if any, creativity (*pillar #4*). When both *pillars* #1 and #4 crumble, the stability of the remaining *pillars* (security and resonance) is threatened as well.

**To summarise**: the wave signal you put out to others, returns to you amplified.

- **Resonance:** if the wave signal is borne of truth, you make your relationships whole - eventually. I'm inclined to quote a phrase, I read on Facebook, *"The truth will set you free but it may p\*\*s you off at first"*. If harsh realities remain not-dealt with then - *"what pesters, festers"*. The issues get worse, often far worse, before they get better. Alternatively, the *bridge* collapses.

- **Dissonance:** if the wave signal is borne of anger, shame, hurt or fear, it will strike the same emotions in others and return to you in amplified waves. If you 'splash the waters' consistently, frequently, strongly and long enough, you may even attract a tsunami to come your way.

Let us assume that you have instilled passion, security and resonance. You are ready to create the last remaining pillar to extend the relationship and go past the outcome you initially set out to achieve together.

## Pillar #4: Creativity

When the relationship/project begins there is a 'Forming and Storming' gestation period (ref: *Appendix 1: The Forming-Storming-Norming-Performing Model of Group Development by Bruce Tuckman*). Hopefully, by building *pillars 1* to *3*, there are few cracks in the relationship and project infrastructure. After, say six months, you start the 'Norming' period. New technologies, systems and working methods are embedded and people begin to experience the new reality that the change team has created for them.

The expertise and management know-how of the recipients of these new systems grows to the extent that they may no longer require the need of outside help in the day-to-day running of operations. If you're some sort of service provider, the management at your client company is now more aware of your working practices and how you make your profit. Your know-how is no longer as scarce a commodity as it was and therefore potentially of less value.

Without some form of creative intervention, you may now expose yourself to:

1. A reduction in the service you provide and/or renegotiation of the terms of the contract, because the gap in skills and knowledge you provide is no longer as large or proprietary to you
2. Some form of client-buy-out clause which savvy customers will have negotiated up front

There's not much you can do to avoid this scenario unless you deliberately block the transfer of wisdom and skills to your customer. Such an activity, I suggest, is not likely to go unnoticed by the client and so the development of a lack of trust, borne of not-truth, develops in the ongoing relationship. *pillars* or their *foundation* may crumble.

If, on the other hand, you build this transferral of wisdom into your plans with the client openly and up front, then you can negotiate terms fairly at the outset and also build in the scope for further reward should you surpass what you set out to achieve.

You may not know precisely at the outset how you are going to generate or unearth new sources of value. Creativity becomes a crucial pillar for people working on the project; a living agenda to identify and establish new opportunities, beneficial to both parties during all four, 'Forming, Storming, Norming and Performing' phases of the project.

Creativity is the art or science of connecting two disparate things to make the something from what was initially thought of as a void.

*Creativity is just connecting things. When you ask creative people how they did something, they feel a little guilty because they didn't really do it, they just saw something. It seemed obvious to them after a while. That's because they were able to connect experiences they've had and synthesize new things. And the reason they were able to do that was that they've had more experiences or they have thought more about their experiences than other people.*

Steve Jobs, the late CEO of Apple

Who would have dreamt that the first internet connections for universities would erupt into a megabillion dollar business woven into the fabric of everyday life?

## Trust - the foundation for success

Whether you're selling or buying, every agreement you make is built around trust.

*Trust is the gap between what you know for fact and whom or what you put faith in.*

I've referred to trust a lot (and truth for that matter). There's a well oiled phrase, *it can take an age to gain someone's trust and a nanosecond to lose it.* Research shows that the biggest single factor that contributes to customer disaffection is lack of trust - when one or both parties lose their trust in the other.

Let's go back to our *bridge* metaphor. It's feasible that during the evolution of a relationship, either party can lose its passion, sense of security, resonance for one another or creativity. One, two, three, even all four of the *pillars of success* may crumble and fall, bringing the overarching structure (pathway to achieving the relationship's purpose) down with them.

It's possible to rebuild those *pillars* but should the *foundations* of the *pillars of success* become unstable, they all stand to crumble and fall, bringing the whole *bridge* down. The *bridge* will not be rebuilt until the *foundation* of trust is re-established. That, in my experience, will not happen in a short period of time.

Trust is vital. Until recent years, I stopped at this point in the business talks I gave. Then one day somebody asked me, *"What about truth? What's the relationship between trust and truth?"* By coincidence (maybe not?), within a few days I started to get some answers from ancient wisdom.

## Truth

Truth comes from the word *Ruth* which in Hebrew is pronounced "root". For a plant to grow and withstand the strongest tempest it must have deep and secure roots. Yet truth is more than the roots or foundation (trust) of a business relationship. It's everywhere.

It's in the *cement* that bonds the *bricks* of the *bridge* together. It's in each *brick*. It's in the plumb line that accords how each *pillar* stands straight. It's at the beginning of the relationship, it's the path you follow to achieve your destination, it's the destination as well. It's in the ethers that flow in between and to-and-from each of the *pillars*. To paraphrase a 60's pop song, "*truth is all around*".

When you veer from truth, you venture into illusion and/or deceit, which manifest in the form of anger, hurt, shame and fear. Should you dispel truth from the relationship you cannot create a truthful outcome. And when one or both parties suspend their belief in the outcome, they start to lose their belief (trust) in the value of one another as a business partner. The relationship might not end there though.

A relationship doesn't end until one or both parties declare that its purpose is complete or no longer achievable. Sometimes, if or when the relationship's purpose is no longer achievable, both parties settle for second best and make good what they can from the relationship. It survives but becomes progressively more moribund.

Why? Because admitting the initial decision to enter into the relationship (that didn't work out as planned) is deemed 'political suicide'. The bigger the decision at the outset, often the more difficult it is to be seen to retract.

By way of example, I've spoken first hand to directors of global corporations who have invested hundreds of millions of dollars in corporate wide programmes (e.g. CRM systems, bespoke sales training systems). Hand-on-heart, they couldn't measure the benefits in a believable fashion. Each was unwilling to question the original decision or purpose for the investment; for fear of the repercussions that such an investigation would cause.

The result: a 'deafening hush' about the investment with the hope it would eventually be brushed under the corporate carpet. The purpose of the investment (i.e. the relationship's true destination) remains but the pathway is no longer there. Perhaps worse still, the opportunity for learning how the original decision led to such a huge setback remains unlearned.

**Truthful completion leads to renewal**

Business relationships don't end by themselves. When their purpose is complete, they end ideally embedded in truth with the foundation of trust still intact. The *pillars* of a successful new relationship can be readily built because the *materials and infrastructure* to build them are already in place.

You could go as far to say that...

*The best time to end a relationship is when its outcomes are complete and both parties are working in perfect harmony with one another - because this is the best time to create stronger partnerships and new outcomes.*

(End of main body of article)

———

## Thank you...

I plan to write further business articles in this *Quick Guide* series. The next has the working title, *Quick Guide IV: A Personal/Corporate Scorecard that Accounts for what Others Fail to Consider* (a simple product and process for CEOs, programme managers and anyone wishing to visualise and measure success).

If you'd like further information about the variety of services I engage in, please visit these websites:

*http://paulcburr.com/* ~ extensive and ethereal blog-site that combines business and ancient wisdom

*http://www.facebook.com/PaulCBurr* ~ over 15,500 followers

*http://twitter.com/paulburr*

*www.cotoco.com* ~ for 'wisdom- transfer' solutions; to pass on what the top performers in your organisation do differently from the 'moderates'

Or mailto: doctapaul@paulcburr.com

# Appendix 1: The Forming-Storming-Norming-Performing Model of Group Development by Bruce Tuckman

In his article, *Developmental Sequence in Small Groups*, written in 1965, Bruce Tuckman defined four phases for a newly formed group (of stakeholders, in the context of this book) to grow, face up to challenges, tackle problems, find solutions, plan work, and ultimately deliver results.

## Phase 1: Forming

Individuals' behaviours are shaped by a desire to be accepted by others, and avoid controversy or conflict. Serious issues and feelings tend to be avoided as individuals gather gathering information and impressions of one another, the scope of the task in hand and how to approach it. This is a comfortable stage to be in but the avoidance of conflict means that any 'hidden truths' are not dealt with.

The first *pillar of success*, passion, may be on the way to being built but it has yet to be 'strength tested'.

## Phase 2: Storming

The group next enter the storming stage in which different ideas compete for consideration. Hidden truths, 'devils in the detail', come to light. Team members open up and confront one another about ideas and perspectives - e.g. how the team should function, who should lead or whom to apportion blame for any mishaps or mistakes.

It can be contentious, unpleasant and painful to members of the team who are averse to conflict. During this phase, the first *pillar of success*, passion, comes under duress and when so, threatens the development of the three remaining *pillars*, security, resonance and creativity.

## Phase 3: Norming

The group eventually agrees on the overarching purpose for coming together; the *bridge's* destination and a mutual plan to get there. Some individuals may give up their personal desires; to allow the group function as a single entity. Individuals take the responsibility and have the ambition to work collaboratively for the success of the overarching goals.

It is at this stage where the *foundations* and *pillars of success* begin to be constructed.

## Phase 4: Performing

Should the team progress through Phase 3, Norming, it now functions as a unit. Individuals' views may differ but issues are resolved collectively and openly. Dissent is expected and channelled through pre-agreed means. Those with opposing views have sufficient mutual respect to hear one another out. A conscious attempt to add conflicting views to one another is made, instead of one side pitching aggressively against the other.

Individuals have embedded sturdy *pillars of success* in a solid *foundation* of trust (in themselves, one another and the processes to which they adhere) rooted in truth.

The group evolves into a knowledgeable, passionate, secure and resonant unit. The combined energies and wisdom of individuals foster the creativity for the group to overachieve its goals. New members can be inducted into the group through reliable methods. The group can ultimately regenerate itself to build new *bridges* (projects) and recycle through Phases 1-3 rapidly.

―――

# Appendix 2: About me, Paul C Burr

Photo © Stephen Cotterell

I equip people to improve their effectiveness by 30%+ in a matter of weeks, sometimes days.

Business Client: *"I have worked with Paul periodically over the past 8 years to gain solutions to a number of people issues / opportunities. If you are looking for a Personal Coach to make a High Performer / High Performing Team even better (particularly a senior player) – I would not hesitate to recommend him."* - Sandra Ventre, Management Development Director, Reckitt Benckiser (now with Qantas)

Private Client: *"You have been so instrumental in the positive changes in my life, I set quite a few goals, and one by one my goals are being achieved, thanks*

***to you, showing me how."*** - Debbie (via Skype) Cape Town, South Africa.

## The Skills and Passions in Me

*Life doesn't get better by chance; it gets better by change.*

*And change is a journey that's two parts emotional to one part intellectual.*

Most of us don't achieve what we set out to achieve at the first attempt. If the outcomes you sought were down to a purely intellectual exercise then you would have achieved them already - would you not? Whether you're a top or moderate performer (or underperforming right now) - every change you make in life is a journey, two parts emotional to one part intellectual. We are twice as likely to hold ourselves back because of self-imposed emotional blocks as opposed to intellectual problems. Put simply, I equip people to tackle challenging emotional journeys.

Corporate clients use me as a 'business coach', personal clients probably see me as more of an 'energy healer'. In both cases I help clients to release the emotional blocks so that they cultivate and apply their innate willpower, imagination, courage and creativity to achieve the business and personal outcomes they seek.

I have over thirty five years of B2B corporate sales and management experience, sixteen years of which overlap with my business and personal coaching work.

I have a PhD in Statistics and a First Class Honours Degree in Mathematics. I'm qualified as a Master Practitioner in NLP, this/past life regression and hypnotherapy.

I give talks (and appear on talk-in shows) on selling, executive coaching, Neuro-Linguistic Programming (NLP), ancient wisdom, football and more ethereal subjects – sometimes to the same audience!

I write books, blogs and am now partway through a series of business articles based upon my own original research, experience and observations in corporate and small/medium businesses.

I study and practice ancient wisdom, astrology, casting runes, dowsing, the I Ching and the Tarot.

I love listening to music – rock, jazz, country... you name it. I sing a bit too.

I'm a passionate football fan of *Newcastle United Football Club*, in "Geordieland", in The North-East of England.

**My Promise:**

*The material I use is powerful, very powerful. I know of nothing quicker or more effective. It's non-mainstream - which means you get non-mainstream results.*

## The Author in Me

*Quick Guide - How Top Salespeople Sell*

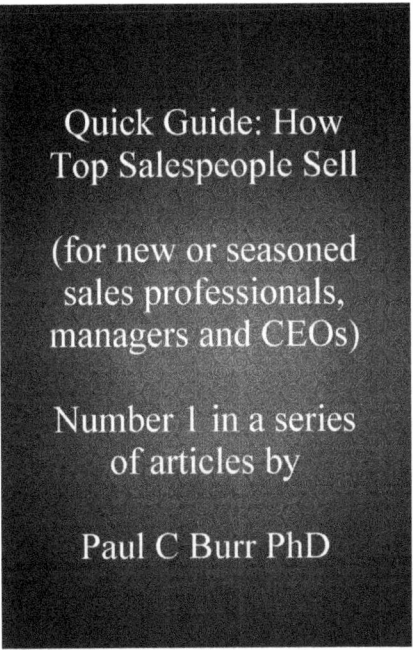

Quick Guide: How Top Salespeople Sell

(for new or seasoned sales professionals, managers and CEOs)

Number 1 in a series of articles by

Paul C Burr PhD

*"...a must read for both novice salespeople and the experienced...."* - Chiahou Zhang, author

*"I loved it... it was great. I've encouraged many of my directors to buy a copy as it's very pertinent to my company"* - paraphrased from a top performing B2B salesperson for a global IT Services organisation

*"I work for a large American IT company, and can say this is a hugely powerful book to articulate what is required to get to Board level. To really understand what the CEO and C level executive*

*summarise as valuable and impactful, and in a condensed easy-to-digest format, is phenomenal. I find Paul C Burr's style of writing easier to digest and apply in any sales situation; it crystallises where the true business value add is delivered and how you really have strategic partnerships. I have just got number 2 book and look forward to reading this with excitement - which is saying something as my concentration span can be limited. Thank you."* - Amy Lambkin, Amazon review

*Quick Guide II - How to Spot, Mimic and Become a Top Salesperson*

Quick Guide II:
How to Spot, Mimic
and Become a Top
Salesperson

(for new or seasoned
sales professionals,
managers and CEOs)

Number 2 in a series of
articles by

Paul C Burr PhD

**Learn to Love and Be Loved in Return**

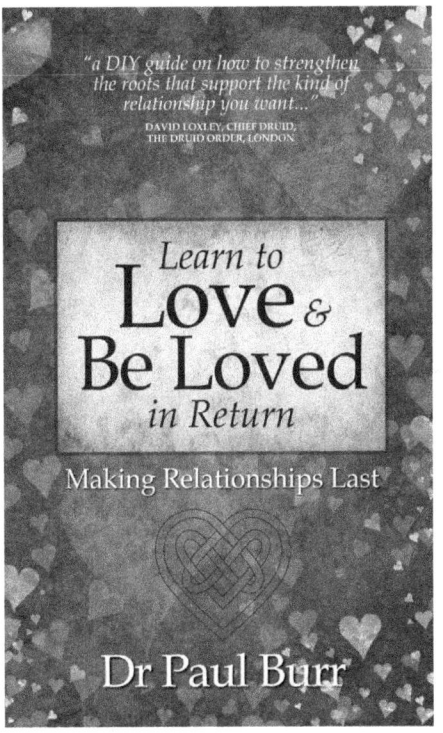

*"Uplifting: this is one of those books that arrives in your life at just the right time, when you need it most. The author is able to convey a very deep and meaningful message in an easy to read and understand format with a step by step guide on how to achieve this. The best type of love is unconditional and what better place to start than with yourself."* - Rhedd, Amazon review

## *2012: a twist in the tail, a novel with spiritual insights*

*"This is a compelling story for our troubled times. Paul C Burr writes with passion and compassion about moral uncertainties and the quest for salvation and spiritual fulfilment. Go with the flow, trust your inner-self and enjoy this humane and optimistic tale."* - Professor John Ditch, York, UK.

*"This is a gripping read - beautiful, insightful and very enjoyable. I found phrases and thoughts staying with me, and becoming part of my understanding of the world."* - Caroline Eveleigh, *Getting to Excellent*

## Defrag your Soul

*"You should be proud of DYS Paul. I think it is amazing and I'm still thinking hard about what you've written."* - Amanda Giles, author

*"DYS whispered to me, 'take heart, be aware, let your journey this far nourish your inner self to be at peace, to love and to shine as your journey continues'."* - Penelope Walsh, book review